ALFRED'S ARTIST SERIES

JACO PASTORIUS

MODERN ELECTRIC BASS

Jaco Pastorious with Jerry Jemmott

CONTENTS

DVD VIDEO ONLINE ACCESS INCLUDED

Stream or download the video content for this book. Please see the enclosed insert card on the inside back cover for more information.

Alfred Music
P.O. Box 10003
Van Nuys, CA 91410-0003
alfred.com

Copyright © MCMXCI, MMVI, MMXVI by Alfred Music
All rights reserved. Printed in USA.
Revised Edition

ISBN-10: 1-4706-3344-2 (Book, DVD & Online Video)
ISBN-13: 978-1-4706-3344-8 (Book, DVD & Online Video)

Interview and text: Jerry Jemmott
Revised edition transcriptions: Lincoln Goines
Additional transcriptions and introduction: Mark Egan
Initial transcriptions: Jerry Jemmott and Kjell Benner
Cover and interior photographs: Ebet Roberts

FOREWORD

The goal of this book is to make the contents of the interview portion of the video, *Jaco Pastorius: Modern Electric Bass*, more accessible to the serious musician who wishes to learn the art of electric bass playing and improvisation. Through the many examples and solos in the book, you will begin to understand the importance of thinking, more than feeling, in the creation of music. Then you will ultimately be able to understand and interpret what you feel, in addition to learning or *re*-learning how to play the electric bass in a very musical way.

The playing of random notes, "wiggling your fingers," doesn't require much thought, whereas the playing of specific patterns does. Just because a phrase or pattern was created with a sixteenth-note feeling doesn't mean that you have to *practice* it at a fast speed. Proceed at your own speed, always using a metronome while practicing the material.

Knowledge of theory, harmony, chord and scale construction, and use of the universal number system of scale steps is a must to facilitate the rapid and thorough learning of your instrument. A brief review is provided for the purpose of memorizing patterns by scale degree or chord quality, interval sequence,

etc. This number system speeds learning, execution, and transposition to other keys and rhythms, in addition to providing a focus for ideas while improvising when accompanying and soloing.

Do yourself a favor! Rewrite the examples from the tape and include at the top of each note its scale degree and chord quality. You will be amazed at how much deeper your understanding will become when this is done. Transcribe the examples and solos yourself, always looking for some kind of pattern. This is excellent for ear training.

Your goal should be to *think fast*, as opposed to *playing fast*. Memorize the patterns by always asking yourself, "what's the pattern, how many times, what is the sequence, which direction (ascending or descending), what's next?"

When you pick up your instrument, always play something specific, such as a chord or arpeggio, part of a scale, song, etc. In other words, have something in mind (tell yourself what to do) and execute it flawlessly, but slowly at first. Good luck! Make it happen!

—Jerry Jemmot

INTRODUCTION

It's very rare for a musician to come along that has the genius and talent to revolutionize the approach to an instrument—Jaco was one of those special individuals.

I was fortunate to have been able to study and play with Jaco both in Miami and on tour with the Gil Evans Orchestra. The energy and feeling with which he approached the music, along with his virtuosity and sound, is what was so inspiring to all of us.

Keep in mind when you're practicing these exercises that it's the *feeling* and *energy* you put into them that really brings the music to life. Use these ideas along with your own imagination to develop your own style of playing.

Thanks, Jaco. Your music lives on in the universe.

—Mark Egan

Western music is based on the chromatic scale out of which the major scale is formed. The major scale is constructed with the following formula: in ascending order; root (1st scale degree), whole-step, whole-step, half-step to the 4th degree, three consecutive whole steps to the 7th degree, and a half-step to the octave to complete the scale

Modal scales are derived from the major scale but start on different degrees, using the same pattern of whole- and half-steps as the major scale. Below are the different modes with their relative chords and their major scale starting points and construction.

Ionian	I	1-2-3-4-5-6-7-8—R-W-W-H-W-W-W-H
Dorian	II	2-3-4-5-6-7-8-2—R-W-H-W-W-W-H-W
Phrygian	III	3-4-5-6-7-8-2-3—R-H-W-W-W-H-W-W
Lydian	IV	4-5-6-7-8-2-3-4—R-W-W-W-H-W-W-W
Mixolydian	V	5-6-7-8-2-3-4-5—R-W-W-H-W-W-H-W
Aeolian	VI	6-7-8-2-3-4-5-6—R-W-H-W-W-H-W-W
Locrian	VII	7-8-2-3-4-5-6-7—R-H-W-W-H-W-W-W

Chords are built on every other note of a major scale such as 1-3-5-7-9-11-13-15 or 2-4-6-8-10-12-14-16. Notes above the first octave are the same as the notes in the first octave, except that they are an octave higher, so that 8=1, 9=2, 10=3, 11=4, etc.

Write out the scales, modes, and chord constructions in reverse order. When transposing to other keys, don't forget to give the proper accidental which will agree with the scale formula you are using.

Chord contruction for ascending 7th chords:

Major	root—major 3rd—minor 3rd—major 3rd
Minor	root—minor 3rd—major 3rd—minor 3rd
Dominant	root—major 3rd—minor 3rd—minor 3rd
Diminished	root—minor 3rd—minor 3rd—minor 3rd
Half-Diminished	root—minor 3rd—minor 3rd—major 3rd
Augmented	root—major 3rd—major 3rd—minor 3rd

If the distance between the root and the 3rd scale degree is two whole-steps (major 3rd), the scale or chord quality is major. If the distance between the root and the 3rd is one and a half-steps (minor 3rd), then the chord or scale is minor.

Diminished chords employ all minor 3rds and the scale construction is W-H-W-H-W-H-W or H-W-H-W-H-W-H-W-H.

o – Let harmonic ring.

✗ – Play as dead note.

◇ – Open diamonds indicate natural harmonics—where they occur indicates finger placement.

● – Filled notes denote standard notes.

D – Strings used are shown below staff.

Numbers used are Jaco's left hand fingering.

Major Scale Modes

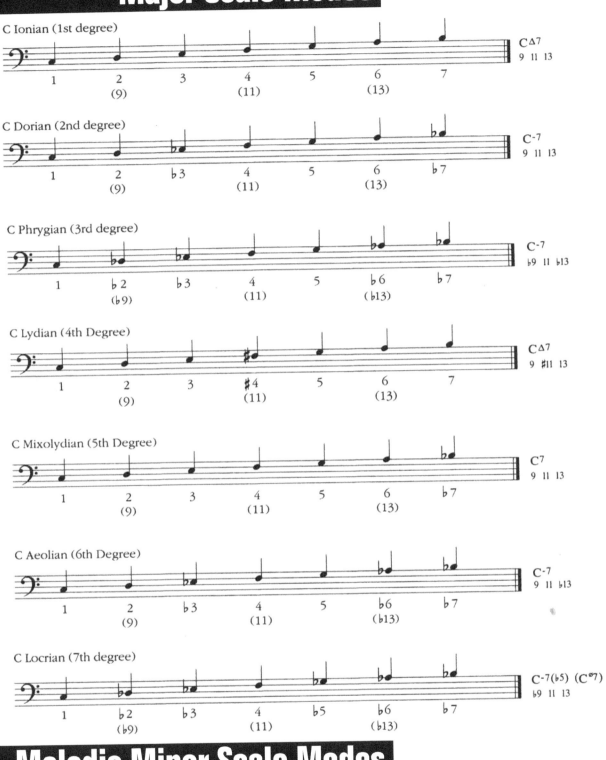

Melodic Minor Scale Modes

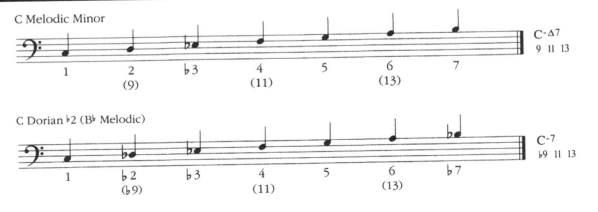

4

C Lydian #5 (A Melodic)

C Lydian ♭7 (G Melodic)

C Mixolydian ♭6 (F Melodic)

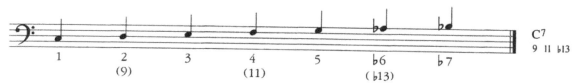

C Locrian #2 (E♭ Melodic)

C Super Locrian (D♭ Melodic)

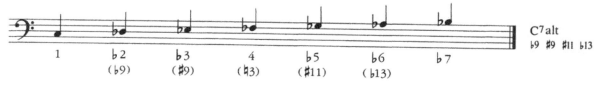

Symmetrical Scales

Diminished

1. C (half-step/whole-step)

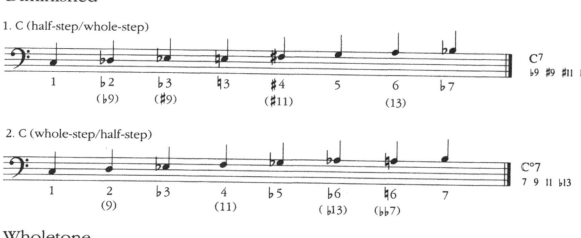

2. C (whole-step/half-step)

Wholetone

C (whole-step/whole-step)

5

EXAMPLE 1—FINGER SPACING—ONE FINGER PER FRET

The chromatic scale is one of the hardest things to play on the bass. Playing it will help teach you where all the notes are through correct finger spacing. Play this scale and all other scales in the following manner: beginning on your low E string, play through one octave and back down; then go through the entire middle and upper register and back down again slowly.

EXAMPLE 2—MAJOR SCALE EXERCISE IN ONE-STRETCH POSITION, USING 16TH-NOTES

This exercise utilizes a descending four-note pattern going down the scale in 2nds.

EXAMPLE 3—ONE OCTAVE MAJOR SCALE IN ASCENDING AND DESCENDING 2NDS

EXAMPLE 4—MAJOR SCALE IN CONSECUTIVE 3RDS AND 2NDS

The numbers at the top of each note represent the degrees used in this pattern. Memorizing the numbers will allow you to "run" the pattern through different keys.

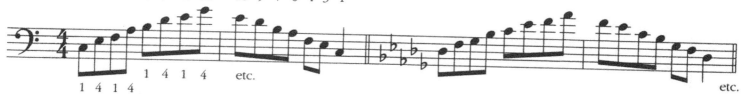

EXAMPLE 5—MAJOR SCALE IN BROKEN 3RDS

This is the "normal" way of playing the scale in 3rds. It is a slower ascent than Jaco's "3rd-2nd" pattern used in example 4.

EXAMPLE 6—ASCENDING MAJOR SCALE IN 2NDS—DESCENDING IN 3RDS— FOLLOWED BY ASCENDING AND DESCENDING IN 3RDS

Notice the pattern used in the first bar, consisting of an ascending major scale in 2nds. The last note of beat 1, bar 2, is the beginning of another series of four-note patterns utilizing descending 7th chord

arpeggios (3rds), moving down the scale in 2nds. Notice how the fourth note of this four-note pattern serves as a pickup, so that the feeling is 4-1-2-3, 4-1-2-3, etc.

EXAMPLE 7—MAJOR SCALE IN 6THS

Scale intervals are used to create sound patterns and to gain awareness of skipping strings and harmonic propulsion.

8

EXAMPLE 8—"JAM IN E"

Thinking ahead with specific ideas is the only way to achieve this level of improvisational clarity and direction.

Slap fingerboard with
palm of right hand - - - - - - - - - -

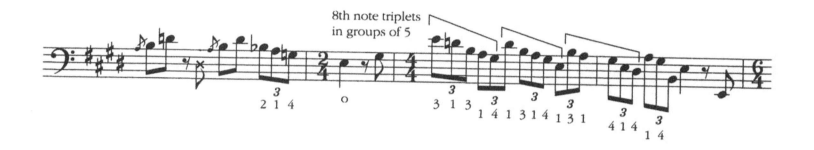

8th note triplets
in groups of 5

Tag

EXAMPLE 9—ARPEGGIOS—FINGERBOARD MEMORIZATION

After you've found where the notes are on the fingerboard—play this exercise without looking to help with memorization of the fingerboard. (With the exception of the octave, the 3rd finger can be substituted for the 4th when playing examples 9 and 10.)

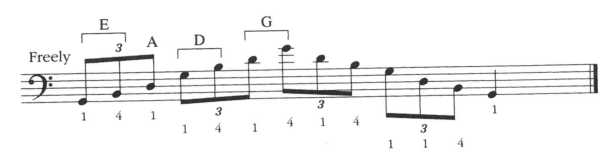

EXAMPLE 10—ARPEGGIOS—ASCENDING CHROMATICALLY

This is the same pattern as example 9—moving up the chromatic scale.

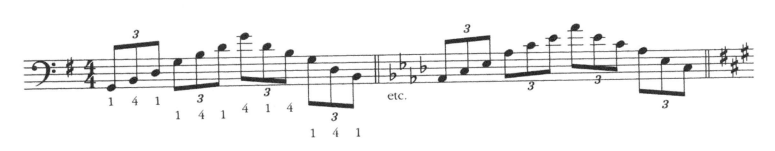

EXAMPLE 11—DOUBLE STOPS

This next example is a very musical approach to playing double stops via spelling out a chord and harmonizing the major scale.

EXAMPLE 12—"THE REAL DEAL"

This next example is based on the ability to create ideas based upon different types of scales, broken arpeggios, chords, and song fragments, all played in patterns utilizing rhythmic groupings.

EXAMPLE 13—MAJOR 7TH ARPEGGIOS

Here's a good exercise: arpeggiate up the I chord, down on the II, up on the III, down on the IV, etc.

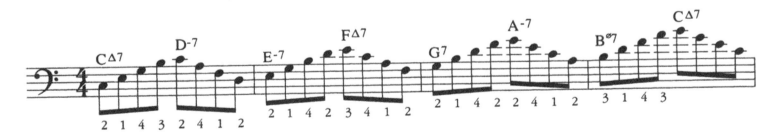

EXAMPLE 14—WHOLE TONE SCALE—ALTERNATING FINGERS

Try going down the scale in 2nds on the downbeat (1-e-an-a)—up the scale in 2nds on the offbeat (e-an-a-1)—down again on the downbeats.

EXAMPLE 15—ALTERNATING FINGERS WITH DIFFERENT NUMBERS

This example shows the division of the beat into five parts—five notes down the scale and up a flatted 5th to the next scale note, a 2nd from the previous starting note.

continue…

EXAMPLE 16—DUET

The use of modes, fingering patterns, rhythm, and chords all become clear when seen on paper. The speed at which it is conceived and executed makes for an exciting sensation for the mind and body.

17

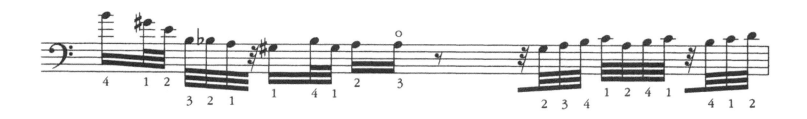

18

19

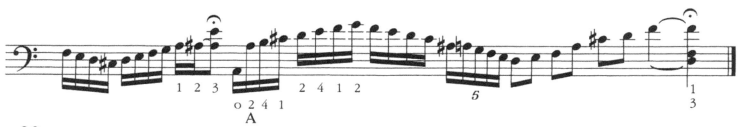

EXAMPLE 17—RIGHT HAND RAKING WITH LEFT HAND MUTING

Practice this example with multiple patterns on even strings. For example: 2nd finger on E, 1st on A, 2nd on D, 1st on G, 1st on E, 3rd on A, 2nd on D, 3rd on G, etc.

EXAMPLE 18—TWO HAND MUTING VIA SCALE IN 3RDS

Be conscious of this very important technique when crossing strings.

EXAMPLE 19—TWO HAND MUTING—EXTENDED

EXAMPLE 20—STRING CROSSING VIA MINOR TO MAJOR CHORDS

Here's something to think about for the left hand and something to do with the right. Try playing this as an open string exercise based on a particular string attack pattern, like in example 17.

Min—1-♭3-5-7-9-11

Maj—1-3-5-7-9-+11

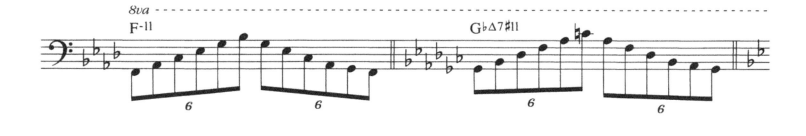

24

EXAMPLE 21—STRING CROSSING IN 4THS

Jaco is actually playing arpeggiated II-V chord progressions—first in 4ths, then chromatically and again in 4ths.

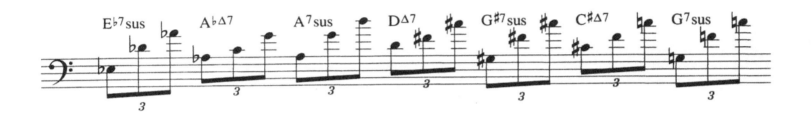

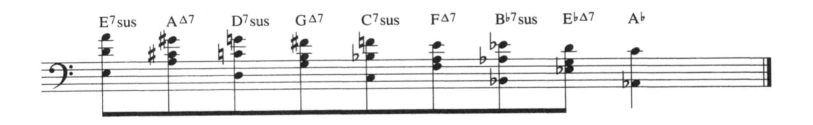

EXAMPLE 22—"BARBARY COAST"

The choice of notes gives it that distinctive sound.

EXAMPLE 23—TUNING THE BASS WITH HARMONICS

This technique ensures accuracy in tuning the bass, owing to the audibility of the notes in this register.

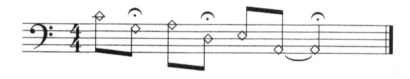

"PORTRAIT OF TRACY" (INTRO)

This example uses harmonics to create a melody.

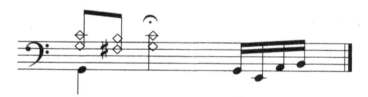

EXAMPLE 24—FALSE HARMONICS—OVERTONE SERIES

This is the division of the string length in halves, quarters, and eighths.

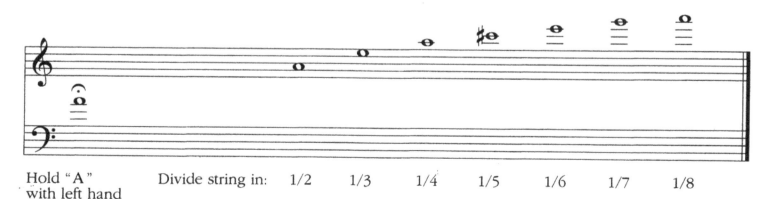

Hold "A" Divide string in: 1/2 1/3 1/4 1/5 1/6 1/7 1/8
with left hand

EXAMPLE 25—FALSE HARMONICS—SCALE IN 3RDS

Divide the string exactly one octave above the fingered note to achieve the harmonic sound quality.

EXAMPLE 26—FALSE HARMONICS USING SCALE PATTERNS AND ARPEGGIOS

Follow the same instructions as in example 25.

EXAMPLE 27—FALSE HARMONICS

Again, follow the same instructions as in example 25.

NATURAL BASS HARMONICS

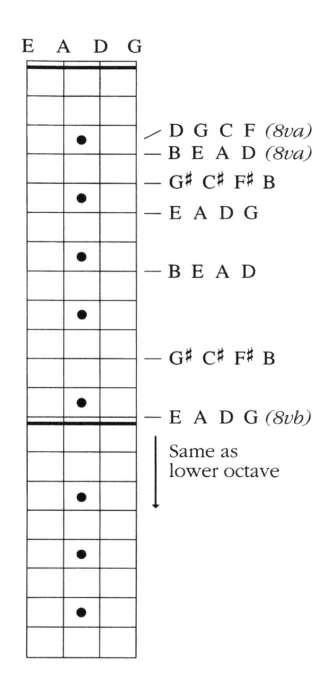

E A D G

— D G C F *(8va)*
— B E A D *(8va)*
— G♯ C♯ F♯ B
— E A D G

— B E A D

— G♯ C♯ F♯ B

— E A D G *(8vb)*

Same as
lower octave

EXAMPLE 28—REMEMBERING "TRACY"

[refer to key on page 3 for notation of harmonics]

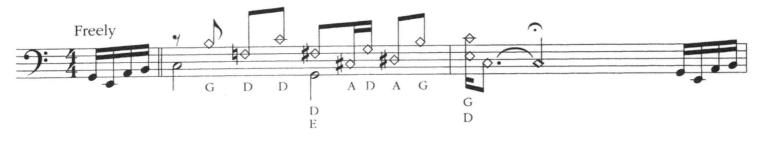

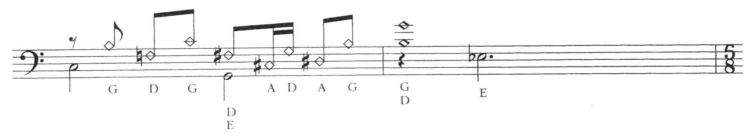

30

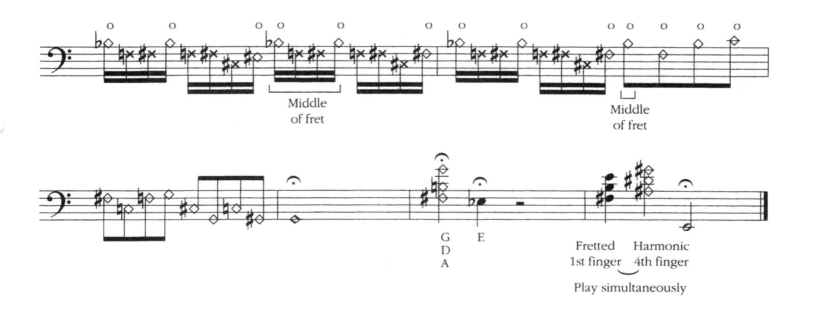

Middle of fret

Middle of fret

G
D
A

E

Fretted   Harmonic
1st finger 4th finger

Play simultaneously

EXAMPLE 29—JERRY'S TIME WITH B.B. KING